Primary Spelling by Pattern

The Greatest Spelling Show on Earth

Level 1

Student Edition

Ellen Javernick, M.A. • Louisa Moats, Ed.D.

Sopris West™
EDUCATIONAL SERVICES

A Cambium Learning Company

BOSTON, MA • LONGMONT, CO

11   B&B   20

ISBN 13-digit: 978-1-60218-476-3
ISBN 10-digit: 1-60218-476-3

Printed in the United States of America

Published and Distributed by

Sopris West™
EDUCATIONAL SERVICES

A Cambium Learning Company

17855 Dallas Parkway, Suite 400 • Dallas, TX 75287 • 800-547-6747
www.voyagersopris.com

(165606/03-19)

Table of Contents

Lesson 1   **Vowel Letters** 1

Lesson 2   **The H Brothers** (Digraphs) 4

Lesson 3   **Vowel Power** (Short-Vowel Sounds) 7

Lesson 4   **Apples** (Short-*a* Words) 10

Lesson 5   **Echoes** (Short-*e* Words) 14

Lesson 6   **Review** (Lessons 1–6) 18

Lesson 7   **The Big Itch** (Short-*i* Words) 21

Lesson 8   **Octopus Hotdogs** (Short-*o* Words) 27

Lesson 9   **Umbrella Up** (Short-*u* Words) 32

Lesson 10   **Sing, Sang, Song** (Word Families) 37

Lesson 11   **By Heart** 42

Lesson 12   **Review** (Lessons 6–11) 44

Lesson 13   **The Floss Pattern** 49

Leson 14   **The Name Game** 56

Lesson 15   **Mr. E's Magic Powers** 61

Lesson 16   **Giant in the City** (Soft *c*) 69

Lesson 17   **Giant in the City** (Soft *g*) 72

Lesson 18   **Review** (Lessons 13–17) 78

Lesson 19   **Shy Guys** (Vowel Teams *ea* and *ee*) 84

Lesson 20   **Shy Guys** (Vowel Teams *oa* and *ai*) 90

Lesson 21   **A Triple Header** (Sounds of Final *y*) 96

Lesson 22   **More and More** (Plurals) 102

Lesson 23   **Let There Be Light** 108

Lesson 24   **Review** (Lessons 19–23) 114

Lesson 25   **Snow Fun** 118

Lesson 26   **The Terrible Twenty** 124

Lesson 27   **Sailboats and Sandboxes** 128

Lesson 28   **Ouch** 134

Lesson 29   **New Moon** 139

Lesson 30   **Cookbook** (o͝o) 144

Lesson 31   **Who Let the Pigs In?** 148

Lesson 32   **Aw, Shucks!** 154

Lesson 33   **Bossy R** 160

Lesson 34   **Final Review** 166

Appendix A: High-Frequency Word List 175

Lesson 1 Vowel Letters

Words and Sounds

Listen to the sentences as your teacher says them. Fill in the missing words and sounds.

1. _____ have _____ ____og.

2. May _____ go ____wimming?

3. The ____ig is in _____ barn.

4. Tom ____ikes soccer and _____ do, too.

5. I had _____ banana for ____unch.

In these sentences, fill in the missing sounds. Some of the missing sounds are at the end of the words.

6. I ca____ ride _____ pony.

7. Did you read _____ goo____ book?

8. Mike and _____ went to the par____.

9. Where did _____ put my ba____?

10. I have _____ red balloo____.

Finding Vowels

Circle the vowels in the following sentence.

The quick brown fox jumps over a lazy dog.

Sound Boxes

After your teacher says a word, move a marker into each box as you say the sounds in the word.

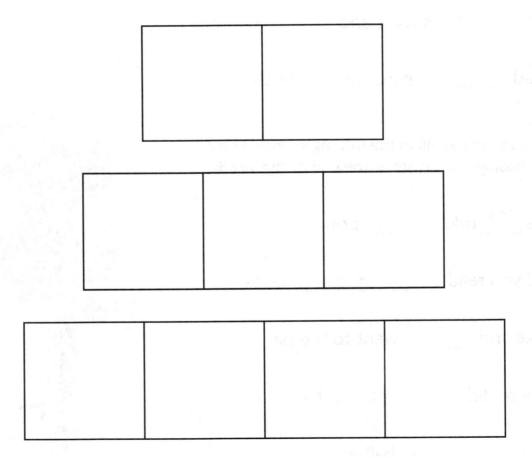

Could It Be a Word?

Every word must have a vowel letter. Fill in the boxes below to show that you know the vowel letters.

					And sometimes

Circle each group of letters that **<u>could</u>** be a word.

chy	blunk	glth	estit
mllrd	obive	shate	pero
hlpr	dunt	hndcfs	grnt
blee	gnwr	blother	sprits
spreng	wrute	sheam	blstd
grank	nvrl	wntr	whum
slust	scnt	timle	mourth

Word Sort: Which Is Which?

Look at the words below. Sort them by digraph.

show	chair	lunch	when	both	slide
trip	chew	show	soap	north	whirl
thumb	catch	mash	ship	where	I

ch	sh	th
	wish	

wh	other	

That's a Good Question

After your teacher says a word, write the letter or letters that begin the word. What question would be a good question to ask?

1. _____ere

2. _____ind

3. _____ich

4. _____ade

5. _____arm

6. _____en

7. _____ipe

8. _____ork

9. _____in

10. _____ith

11. _____eel

12. _____ait

13. _____ay

14. _____ant

15. _____ale

16. _____at

17. _____ite

18. _____ords

19. _____ile

20. _____ould

Do I use wh or w?

Fishing

Read the story and underline or highlight the digraphs **ch**, **sh**, **th**, and **wh**.

One Thursday, Mitch went with his brother Chad to the beach. They took their fishing rods because they hoped to catch a batch of fish.

When they left, the weather was beautiful and the sun was shining. They both waded into the shallow water. They threw in their lines. Mitch thought there was something on his line. He pulled it through the water. It was not a fish. It was a branch.

Just then Chad's line shook. "I think I've hooked something big," he whispered. "It's much too big to be a fish. It feels like a whale or a shark." He clutched his rod tightly. Chad and Mitch worked together to pull the fish to the shore. It was a thirty-pound catfish with bushy whiskers.

"I think we should let it go," said Mitch. Chad watched while Mitch took the hook out of the fish's mouth and threw it back into the water. The brothers did not get to fish any more that day because just then it began to thunder. They hurried home to eat their lunch.

The Short-Vowel Song

Hear the sound of

/ă/ **apple**

/ĕ/ **echo**

/ĭ/ /ĭ/ **itch**

/ŏ/ /ŏ/ /ŏ/ /ŏ/ **octopus**

and /ŭ/ **umbrella**, too.

Short Vowels

Write the letters you hear your teacher say.

1. _____

2. _____

3. _____

4. _____

5. _____

6. _____

7. _____

The letter a can have two sounds: a schwa sound and /ă/."

Next, write the letters for the vowel sounds you hear in the words your teacher says.

8. _____

9. _____

10. _____

11. _____

12. _____

13. _____

14. _____

15. _____

16. _____

Spelling in Sound Boxes

Say the sounds of the word. Write the letter or letters that spell each sound in a box. Color the vowels when you are finished.

Every word contains a vowel.

1	m	o	p	11.			
2				12.			
3				13.			
4				14.			
5				15.			
6				16.			
7				17.			
8				18.			
9				19.			
10				20.			

Lesson 4 Apples (Short-*a* Words)

Read and Copy
Read the words, then copy them on the lines provided.

1. can   can _____

2. and   _____

3. at   _____

4. had   _____

5. an   _____

6. that   _____

7. has   _____

8. than   _____

9. ran   _____

10. am   _____

11. fast   _____

12. ask   _____

13. as   _____

14. sad   _____

15. nap   _____

16. sat   _____

17. man   _____

18. mad   _____

19. lap   _____

20. bag   _____

21. dad   _____

22. mat   _____

23. pat   _____

24. wag   _____

25. cat   _____

26. bat   _____

27. wax   _____

28. van   _____

Primary Spelling by Pattern Student

Finding *a* Words

Read the story. Highlight the letter **a** where you find it.

Matt and Sam

Matt has a cat. The cat is Sam. Matt has a van. Matt and Sam go in the van. In the van, Sam has a mat. Sam will not go on the mat. Sam will go on Matt's lap. Matt pats Sam. Sam is glad.

Dictation

Write the words, phrases, or sentences your teacher says.

_____

1. _____
   _____

2. _____
   _____

3. _____
   _____

4. _____
   _____

5. _____
   _____ _____ _____

6. _____ _____ _____
   _____ _____ _____

7. _____ _____ _____ _____
   _____ _____ _____

8. _____ _____ _____ _____.
   _____ _____ _____ _____

9. _____ _____ _____ of _____.
   _____ _____ _____

10. _____ _____ _____ _____
    _____ _____
    _____ _____.

Word Families: Words You Didn't Know You Knew

Write words that belong in the same word family.

1. **ant**

   pant
   _____
   _____
   _____

2. **wag**

   tag
   _____
   _____
   _____

3. **sad**

   _____
   _____
   _____
   _____

4. **tap**

   _____
   _____
   _____
   _____

5. **camp**

   _____
   _____
   _____
   _____

6. **fat**

   _____
   _____
   _____
   _____

7. **and**

   _____
   _____
   _____
   _____

8. **jam**

   _____
   _____
   _____
   _____

9. **cash**

   _____
   _____
   _____
   _____

Listen for all consonant sounds in the word. Remember that the letters sh make just one sound.

Lesson 5 Echos (Short-*e* Words)

Read and Copy
Read the words, then copy them on the lines provided.

1. get

2. them

3. then

4. when

5. red

6. let

7. best

8. yes

9. help

10. well

11. ten

12. set

13. men

14. jet

15. vet

16. bed

17. send

18. spent

19. step

20. hen

21. desk

22. self

23. melt

24. mend

25. fresh

26. rest

27. leg

28. egg

Finding Short-*e* Words in Context

Read the story and highlight the /ĕ/ words.

Beth and Ben and the Red Hen

Beth and Ben have a pet hen. Beth and Ben have Red. Red is not well.

Mom and Beth and Ben and Red get in the van. "We will go to the vet,"

Mom tells Beth and Ben.

Beth tells the vet, "Red is not well."

The vet tells Ben, "It is not too bad.

Red will get well."

Mom thanks the vet and gets Red in the

van. "We will go home now," Mom tells

Beth and Ben.

Back home at last, Ben lets Red into her pen. Red gets fed. She pecks

and pecks.

Fill in the Blanks

After you read the story, fill in the words that make sense.

1. Beth and Ben have a _____ _____ .

2. Mom, Beth, and Ben _____ in _____ van.

3. The _____ tells Ben that the hen will get

   _____ .

Word Families: **Words You Didn't Know You Knew**

Write some more words for the word families below.

1. **heck**

   deck
   _____
   _____
   _____

2. **bed**

   red
   _____
   _____
   _____

3. **bell**

   _____
   _____
   _____

4. **belt**

   _____
   _____
   _____

5. **den**

   _____
   _____
   _____

6. **sent**

   _____
   _____
   _____

7. **slept**

   _____
   _____
   _____

8. **mess**

   _____
   _____
   _____

9. **wet**

   _____
   _____
   _____

If you hear more than one consonant sound, you need to write more than one consonant.

Lesson 6 Review (Lessons 1–6)

Spelling in Sound Boxes

Write the words your teacher dictates in the sound boxes.

Are there some words that are fair to ask about?

1	m	a	d	11.			
2	sh			12.			
3				13.			
4				14.			
5				15.			
6				16.			
7				17.			
8				18.			
9				19.			
10				20.			

Vowel Bingo Card

Put a vowel letter in every box on your vowel Bingo card, below.

V	O	W	E	L

Sentence Writing

Use words from the Word Bank to write sentences.

Word Bank

can	and	at	had	send	as	men
an	that	has	than	desk	Dad	mad
ran	am	fast	ask	self	well	
them	then	when	red	fresh	ten	
let	best	yes	help	sad	went	

1. _____

_____

2. _____

_____

3. _____

_____

4. _____

_____

5. _____

_____

Hear the Difference

Point to the picture that matches the vowel sound in the word your teacher says.

Read and Copy

Read the words, then copy them on the lines provided.

1. this   this
2. did
3. him
4. with
5. which
6. big
7. wish
8. six
9. his
10. bit
11. ship
12. swim
13. grin
14. chip
15. strip

16. lit
17. win
18. crib
19. hid
20. rip
21. lift
22. mist
23. crisp
24. win
25. kid
26. miss
27. trip
28. wilt
29. slid
30. is

Changing the Vowel to Make a New Word

Change the **e** in each of these words into an **i**. Read the new word you make.

1. sled   <u>slid</u>

2. pen   _____

3. set   _____

4. beg   _____

5. let   _____

6. pet   _____

7. bet   _____

8. bed   _____

9. ten   _____

10. red   _____

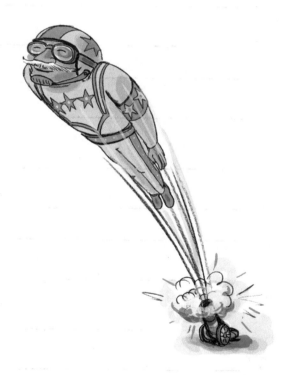

Sentence Dictation

Listen to the following sentences and write the words on the lines.

1. _____ _____ _____ _____ _____ ___

   _____ ___ _____ _____ , ___

   _____ _____ _____ _____

   _____ _____ _____ _____ .

2. ___ _____ _____ _____ _____

   _____ _____ _____ _____

   _____

   _____ .

3. _____ _____ _____ _____ _____

   _____ _____ _____ _____ _____

   _____

   _____ .

4. _____ _____ _____ _____ _____

   _____ _____ _____ _____ _____

   _____ _____ _____ _____ ?

5. _____ _____ _____ _____ _____

   _____ _____ _____

   _____ _____ .

Finding *i* Words

Read the story. Find and highlight the words with the short-**i** vowels.

Let's Fish

"Can we go fish?" Bill and Tim ask Dad.

Dad grins. "Yes, we will go fish in the ditch by the hill. We will let Wags go too. I will fix a picnic and fill the van with gas. Then we will go."

"I will catch a big fish," says Bill. "It will be bigger than six inches."

"I will catch a bigger fish," says Tim.

"If you do not quit that, we will not fish," says Dad.

At last, Dad and the kids get to the ditch. They sit still and fish. Tim catches a stick. Bill catches a red rag.

Wags will not sit still. He gets wet. Then he gets Dad and the kids wet. "Wags is a pill," says Tim.

I do not think fish live in this ditch," says Bill.

We cannot grill fish," says Dad. "But we can still have a picnic. We will have chips and ham sandwiches. We will not miss the fish!"

Word Families: Words You Didn't Know You Knew

Write some more words for the word families below.

1. **p<u>ick</u>**

   sick
   _____
   _____
   _____

2. **k<u>id</u>**

   _____
   _____
   _____
   _____

3. **w<u>ill</u>**

   _____
   _____
   _____
   _____

4. **br<u>im</u>**

   _____
   _____
   _____
   _____

5. **bl<u>imp</u>**

   _____
   _____
   _____
   _____

6. **ch<u>in</u>**

   _____
   _____
   _____
   _____

7. **m<u>iss</u>**

   _____
   _____
   _____
   _____

8. **s<u>it</u>**

   _____
   _____
   _____
   _____

9. **d<u>ish</u>**

   _____
   _____
   _____
   _____

If we hear more than one consonant sound, we need to write more than one consonant.

Lesson 8 Octopus Hot Dogs (Short-*o* Words)

Read and Copy

Read the words below, then copy them.

Ask for help when you're not sure whether to use a short-o or an "aw shucks" combination.

1. not _____

2. stop _____

3. hot _____

4. got _____

5. jog _____

6. box _____

7. hop _____

8. job _____

9. lot _____

10. sob _____

11. pop _____

12. odd _____

13. sock _____

14. pond _____

15. shock _____

16. pot _____

17. frog _____

18. rock _____

19. clock _____

20. chomp _____

21. shop _____

22. trot _____

23. lock _____

24. blot _____

Sentence Dictation

Listen to the following sentences and write the words on the lines.

1. _____ _____ _____ _____

   _____ _____ _____ _____

   _____ _____ _____ _____

2. _____ _____ _____ _____

   _____ _____ _____ _____

   _____ _____ _____

3. _____ _____ _____ _____ _____

   _____ _____

   _____ _____

4. _____ _____ _____ _____ _____

   _____ _____ _____ _____

   _____ _____ _____

5. _____ _____ _____ _____ _____

   _____ _____ _____

   _____ _____ _____

Alphabetical Order

a b c d e f g h i j k l m n o p q r s t u v w x y z

Look at the first letter of each word. Put the words in order of the alphabet.

friend	chick	his	job
the	of	which	rock

1. _____

2. _____

3. _____

4. _____

5. _____

6. _____

7. _____

8. _____

Finding Short *o* Words in Context

Read the story and highlight the words with /ŏ/.

A Friend for Ollie

Ollie Octopus felt sad. He did not have a friend. He asked his mom if it was OK to swim off to get a friend.

"Yes," said his mom, "but be back by six o'clock."

"OK," said Ollie and off he swam. He met a frog on top of a rock. "Let's be friends," said Ollie.

"No," said the frog, and he hopped off.

Ollie got to a spot filled with a lot of codfish. When Ollie said, "Let's be friends," the codfish swam off.

At last, a big squid shot past Ollie. "Stop!" said Ollie. "Will you be my friend?"

The squid nodded. "Yes," he said. "I will be glad to have an octopus for a friend."

Sound-Alikes

Underline the right spelling of the word in the sentences.

When you mean more than one of something, use the ks spelling at the end of a word.

1. When the (**clocks/clox**) stopped, I had to set them.

2. Dad hit the log with his (**ax/acks**).

3. Mom has snacks in the (**pax/packs**).

4. The dog can do ten (**trix/tricks**).

5. The ship had six (**decks/dex**).

6. Ben can (**mix/micks**) the dish of ham and eggs.

7. (**Macks/Max**) got his feet wet in the pond.

8. The Jack-in-the-(**box/bocks**) had a red pom-pom on its hat.

9. I will toss the (**stix/sticks**) for the big dogs.

10. Can you cash the (**checks/chex**) at the bank?

Lesson 9 Umbrella Up (Short-*u* Words)

Read and Copy

Read and copy the words.

1. cut

2. must

3. fun

4. pup

5. mud

6. gun

7. sun

8. drum

9. snug

10. dump

11. stuck

12. puff

13. gulp

14. lunch

15. bunch

16. brush

17. plump

18. stump

19. hunt

20. hush

21. trust

22. shut

23. up

24. but

25. just

26. run

27. us

28. much

Story Dictation

Listen, repeat, and write the sentences in the story about Wags.

Wags

_____ _____ ___ _____

....

_____ _____ _____

___ ___ ___ ___

....

_____. ____ ____ said, " _____

....

_____ _____ " _____ _____

....

_____, _____ . _____ _____

_____ _____ _____ _____ _____

....

_____ _____ _____ ___, ___

_____ _____ _____ ___ _____

....

_____ _____ ___ _____ _____.

" _____ _____ " _____

....

_____ ___, " said _____ .

_____ _____ _____ _____

....

_____ _____ ___ _____.

_____ _____ ___ !

....

_____ _____ ___ !

Rhymes

Complete the rhyme and check the answer to the question.

	Yes	No

1. Can you buy <u>chops</u> at sh_____? ☐ ☐

2. Can you put a <u>fish</u> on a d_____? ☐ ☐

3. Can you drink <u>punch</u> for l_____? ☐ ☐

4. Do you make a <u>mess</u> when you play ch_____? ☐ ☐

5. Can you do <u>math</u> while you take a b_____? ☐ ☐

6. Do you hear a <u>gush</u> when you fl_____? ☐ ☐

Finding Short-*u* Words in Context

Read the story and highlight the /ŭ/ words.

Fun at Camp

Judd hugged his Mom and Dad. He patted his pup. Then he got on a bus. He went to camp. Judd slept on a bunk bed in a tent. He went to the pond to swim. At lunch he had punch. He had buns, and he got crumbs for the ducks. A bunch of bugs bit him, but he did not fuss. The camp had a tramp, and Judd jumped on it. Just at dusk, Judd felt wet drops. He ran fast to his tent. He just got a bit damp. Judd and the rest of the kids had a lot of fun at the camp.

Write a sentence that tells about Judd at camp.

_____

_____

_____

_____

_____

Word Families: **Words You Didn't Know You Knew**

Write words that rhyme to make a word family.

1. **bug**

   rug

2. **drum**

3. **grump**

4. **munch**

5. **brush**

6. **shut**

If we hear more than one consonant sound, we need to write more than one consonant.

Primary Spelling by Pattern Student

Lesson 10 Sing, Sang, Song (Word Families)

Word Sort: A Slick Magic Trick

Write each word from the word list in the correct hat.

□ck

peek silk talk snack park slick make
spank ask speck week chick hike
pink disk neck yuck hulk

Vowel Is Not Short	Short Vowel + Two Consonant Sounds	Short Vowel + /k/
1. _peek_	1. _silk_	1. _snack_
2. _____	2. _____	2. _____
3. _____	3. _____	3. _____
4. _____	4. _____	4. _____
5. _____	5. _____	5. _____
6. _____	6. _____	6. _____

Sentence Dictation

Repeat each sentence and write the words.

1. _____ _____ _____ _____ _____ _____
   _____
   _____ .

2. He _____ _____ _____ _____ _____
   C___er _____ _____ .

3. _____ _____ _____ _____ _____ _____
   _____ _____ _____ _____
   _____ _____ _____ _____
   _____ _____ _____ _____ .

4. _____ _____ _____ to _____ _____
   _____ _____ _____ _____ _____
   _____ _____
   _____ _____ .
   _____ _____ _____ _____ _____

5. _____ _____ _____ _____ _____ _____
   _____
   _____ .

Letter Detective

As quickly as you can, find and circle all the words with □**ck**. Then, read the silly sentences.

1.

Nick did a slick magic trick when he pulled a duck out of a black hat.

2.

Yuck! Do not lick that. You will get sick.

3.

Ask Dad when the clock tells him to get up.

Word Sort

Sort the words in the word list by their last three letters: **ing**, **ang**, or **ong**.

Word List

ring	bring	bang	dong	strong	swing	hang
fang	long	wrong	thing	gang	gong	slang
spring	king	wing	sprang	throng	rang	ping-pong

sing

1. ring
2. _____
3. _____
4. _____
5. _____
6. _____
7. _____

sang

1. _____
2. _____
3. _____
4. _____
5. _____
6. _____
7. _____

song

1. _____
2. _____
3. _____
4. _____
5. _____
6. _____
7. _____

Match the ending sound with the sound in the note.

Word Sort: Honk If You Know the Pattern

Sort the words by the pattern they follow. The first one is done for you.

Word List

tank	stink	honk	pink	think
drank	blank	prank	trunk	bonk
bunk	mink	zonk	skunk	junk

bank

1. _____

2. _____

3. _____

4. _____

rink

1. _____

2. _____

3. _____

4. _____

hunk

1. _____

2. _____

3. _____

4. _____

bonk

1. _____

2. _____

3. _____

Lesson 11 By Heart

Question Word Clues

Read these memory sentences and learn the clues.

1. **who**   Who says *whooo*?

2. **what**   What **hat** will you wear?

3. **where**   Where is it? **Here** it is.

4. **when**   When will the **hen** lay the egg?

5. **why**   Why did you **cry**?

Dictation

Write the question words below.

1. _____   4. _____

2. _____   5. _____

3. _____

Word Choice: *a* or *an*

Decide whether **a** or **an** should be used before each word. Write the correct word on the line.

1. _____ apple

2. _____ friend

3. _____ table

4. _____ girl

5. _____ umbrella

6. _____ octopus

7. _____ chair

8. _____ whale

9. _____ echo

10. _____ itch

11. _____ egg

12. _____ fish

Remember to use a before a consonant sound and an before a vowel sound.

Lesson 12 Review (Lessons 6–11)

Spelling in Sound Boxes

One box stands for one sound. Say each word. Stretch the sounds. For each sound, write the letter(s) in a sound box.

1	s	i	ck	
2				
3				
4				
5				
6				
7				
8				
9				
10				
11				
12				
13				
14				
15				
16				

Sentence Completion

Listen and write in the right word.

Last weekend, my friend _____ ran into a _____ on the path. His eyes _____ from the _____. He felt _____. Mick went _____ to his mom as _____ as he could. Yuck!

Which Question Word?

What question word belongs at the beginning of each sentence? Answer the question after you write the question word.

_____ was Mick? _____

_____

_____ was he? _____

_____

_____ did he run into? _____

_____

_____ way did he run? _____

_____

_____ did he meet the skunk? _____

_____

Alphabetical Order

a b c d e f g h i j k l m n o p q r s t u v w x y z

Look at the first letter of each word. Put the words in order of the alphabet.

every	could	many	friend	words	about
of	you	people	been	do	said

1. _____

2. _____

3. _____

4. _____

5. _____

6. _____

7. _____

8. _____

9. _____

10. _____

11. _____

12. _____

Story Dictation

Write the story your teacher dictates.

_____ _____ ___ ___ ___

_____ _____ ___ ___ ___

_____ ____ ___ ___ ____

____ _____ • _____

_____ _____ ___ ___ __ ___

_____ ____ __ _____, ___ ___

____ _____ _____ _____

____. _____ _____ ____ ____ed

____ ____ ___ ___ __

_____ _____ _____• ____

____ ____ed, "____ ____! __ ___ my

____ " ____ ___ ___ ___

____. ____ ____ ____ ___

____ ____ ___ ___ ___

____ _____ _____

____ _____ •

Heart Word Review

Write the Heart Words your teacher says.

Floss Words

Underline the letter that comes right before **ff**, **ll**, or **ss**. Then read the word.

ll

smell

still

doll

ff

staff

off

cliff

ss

class

mess

kiss

Don't forget
to floss!

Finding Floss Words in Context

Read the story. Highlight all the Floss words, including those with *ed* at the end.

Prince Ross

The king huffed and puffed up the hill. At the top, he rang his big brass bell. Bong! Bong! Bong! A lot of people ran to the hill. Tess ran to the hill, too.

"I will tell you why I rang my bell," said the king. "I must pick a lass to wed my son Ross. He is a bit of a pill, but I still love him. I will pick him a lass who will let him be boss. She will pick up his mess. She will dress up and sit still. She will not tell Ross off. She will fill up his glass and grill bass for his lunch. When he is full, she will get him his chess set and a lap rug so he will not get a chill."

Then the King said to Tess, "I pick you to wed Ross. You must be thrilled!"

"Well, I am **not** thrilled," said Tess.

Just then Ross ran up to kiss Tess.

"Yuck," said Tess. "You did not floss. You smell!" Tess ran from Ross.

"Stop, Miss," yelled Ross. "I will brush and I will floss and I will let you be boss if you will wed me."

"No thanks," said Tess, "but I do wish you well, and I will still be your friend."

Word Sort: Floss Words

Sort the words from the word list. Write them under the teeth according to their last letters.

Word List

sniff	gruff	chill	spell	glass	kiss	tell
whiff	press	floss	spill	as	cliff	puff
huff	bell	if	stress	grill	off	well
toss	less	stuff	hill	brass	this	yes

ff

1. _____
2. _____
3. _____
4. _____
5. _____
6. _____
7. _____
8. _____

ll

1. _____
2. _____
3. _____
4. _____
5. _____
6. _____
7. _____
8. _____

ss

1. _____
2. _____
3. _____
4. _____
5. _____
6. _____
7. _____
8. _____

1. _____   2. _____   3. _____

4. _____

Pick a Pattern

Read the spelling patterns. Beside each word in the word list, write the number or numbers of the patterns that are used to spell it. The first one is done for you.

Spelling Patterns

1. The short **a** sound is usually spelled with the single letter **a**.

2. The short **e** sound is usually spelled with the single letter **e**.

3. The short **i** sound is usually spelled with the single letter **i**.

4. The short **o** sound is usually spelled with the single letter **o**.

5. The short **u** sound in a short word or after a consonant in the first syllable of a longer word is usually spelled with the single letter **u**.

6. When we hear two or three consonant sounds together in a word, we spell them all.

7. When a final /k/ sound directly follows a short vowel sound, we spell it **ck**.

8. The **ch**, **sh**, **th**, **wh**, and **ng** sounds are spelled with two letters.

9. In a single-syllable word, when a final **f**, **l**, or **s** directly follows a short vowel sound, we usually double the **f**, **l**, or **s**.

10. The five question words start with **wh**.

11. Some words do not follow patterns and we just have to memorize them.

Words

1. slick   Patterns 3, 6, and 7

2. kiss

3. champ

4. ask

5. spend   _____

6. when   _____

7. dump   _____

8. list   _____

9. the   _____

10. spell   _____

11. shed   _____

12. sand   _____

13. bring   _____

14. with   _____

15. was   _____

16. sock   _____

17. melt   _____

18. puff   _____

Sentence Dictation

Write the sentences your teacher says.

It's fair to ask if cannot is one word or two.

1. _____ _____ _____ _____ _____
_____ _____ _____ _____
_____ _____ _____ _____ .

2. _____ _____ _____ _____ _____ _____
_____ _____ _____ _____ _____
_____ _____ _____ , _____ _____ _____ _____ .

3. _____ _____ _____ _____ _____
_____ _____ _____ , _____ _____
_____ _____ _____ _____ _____
_____ _____ _____ _____ .

4. _____ said, " _____ _____ _____
_____ _____ _____ _____ ,
_____ _____ _____ _____ "
_____ , _____ _____ _____ _____ .

5. _____ _____ _____ _____ _____ _____
_____ _____
_____ _____ .

Primary Spelling by Pattern Student

6. _____ said, "_____ _____ _____

_____ _____ _____ _____ "

_____ _____ _____ _____ .

7. _____ _____ _____ _____ _____

_____ _____ _____ _____ _____

_____ _____ _____

_____ _____ _____ .

8. _____ _____ _____ _____ _____ _____

_____ _____ _____ _____ _____

_____ _____ _____ _____

_____ _____ _____ .

9. _____ _____ _____ _____ _____ _____

_____ _____ _____ _____ _____

_____ _____ _____ _____ _____

_____ _____ _____ _____ .

10. _____ _____ _____ _____ _____ , _____

_____ _____ _____ _____ _____

_____ _____ _____ _____ .

Memory Pictures

Draw a picture of a cue word that will help you remember each long-vowel sound.

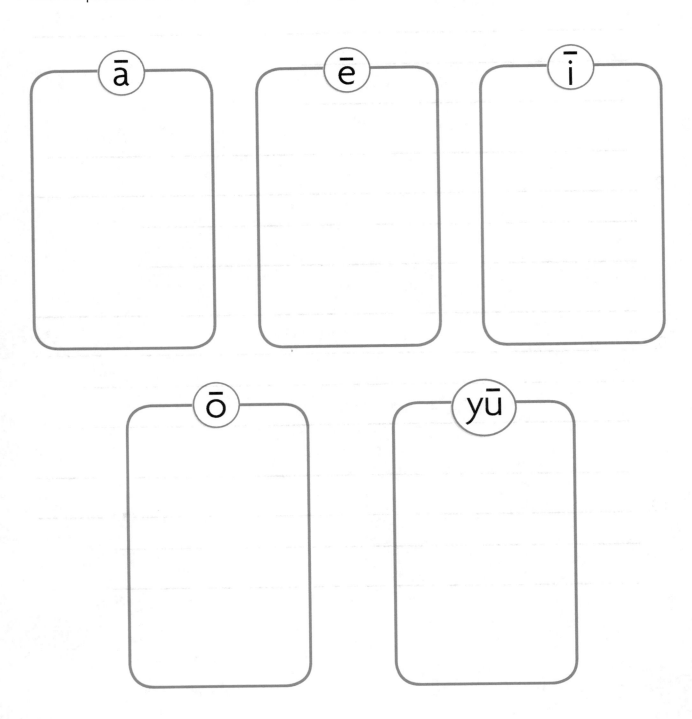

Speed Read: Question Words

Get ready to read these words as quickly as you can.

where	which	why	who	what	when
why	which	what	when	who	where
when	why	who	which	where	what
why	where	when	what	which	who
when	what	who	which	where	why
what	who	where	why	which	when
who	where	when	what	which	why

My Score

_____ words correct in one minute.

Write the question words:

1. _____

2. _____

3. _____

4. _____

5. _____

Short Words With Long-Vowel Sounds

Write each word two times. Say the word as you write.

me   _____   _____

go   _____   _____

he   _____   _____

so   _____   _____

she   _____   _____

no   _____   _____

we   _____   _____

be   _____   _____

Make hearts for these words:

to   do

Primary Spelling by Pattern Student

Seeing Is Believing

Look carefully at the three spellings while your teacher says a word. Only one is spelled correctly. When you find the correct spelling, circle it.

1.	frend	frende	friend
2.	hoo	who	whu
3.	family	famale	famile
4.	wus	wuz	was
5.	why	whi	wie
6.	uv	ov	of
7.	spel	spell	speel
8.	champ	shamp	camp
9.	duk	duc	duck
10.	whut	wut	what
11.	the	thu	they
12.	wif	with	wiv
13.	truck	chruck	truk
14.	spring	sprin	sprig
15.	bank	banck	banc

Word Find

Circle the 20 "unfair" words hidden in the puzzle.

Word List

what	of	who	only	friend	went	where	first	some	want
many	was	family	they	said	with	people	been	water	were

```
B   E   F   W   H   O   L   W   O   F   M   B
N   T   A   H   B   N   S   R   A   R   C   R
W   L   X   A   K   L   X   F   F   I   O   P
W   E   N   T   K   Y   W   R   Y   E   Y   S
P   T   W   H   E   R   E   O   X   N   B   A
F   I   R   S   T   S   O   M   E   D   B   T
L   M   W   A   N   T   G   Z   D   X   W   I
F   A   M   I   L   Y   H   A   W   M   P   T
C   H   H   D   P   P   H   R   W   A   S   R
F   C   P   L   L   B   D   A   L   N   L   X
P   E   O   P   L   E   T   H   E   Y   D   W
S   C   U   R   R   E   L   P   T   Z   B   I
M   K   Y   K   S   N   S   B   G   G   R   T
W   A   T   E   R   G   W   E   R   E   W   H
```

Poem

Read the following poem with your teacher.

Mr. E

Mr. E. has super powers.

He keeps us entertained for hours.

He puts words into his hat,

waves his wand, and just like that,

    pin becomes **pine**

    twin becomes **twine**.

He drops in **mat** and pulls out **mate**,

Mr. E. is really great.

He can turn **hop** to **hope**.

He even changes **cop** to **cope**.

If he really concentrates,

rats turns right into **rates**.

When he pays his magician dues,

He changes **us** straight into **use**.

Invite Mr. E to visit you

and see the fine things he can do.

Read and Copy

Write the words in the magician's hat on the lines below.

bite   nose

use

trade   late   blame

smile   cute   glide

shake

1. _____   6. _____

2. _____   7. _____

3. _____   8. _____

4. _____   9. _____

5. _____   10. _____

Read and Copy

1. same

2. drove

3. home

4. white

5. whale

6. bake

7. slide

8. size

9. shine

10. bite

11. spine

12. code

13. mine

14. lake

15. stripe

16. shake

17. hide

18. ripe

19. life

20. made

21. line

22. bride

23. here

24. cube

25. dive

26. rode

VCe Hunt

Highlight or underline each VCe word that you find in the story below. Read the story aloud.

Dad's Cake

When Jane and Pete woke up, Mom said, "Let's take a trip to the store. This is a fine time to get things to make a lime cake for Dad."

"Will we hike, skate, or ride bikes?" asked Pete.

"We will use bikes," said Mom. She wrote a note. It said:

eggs

cake mix

lime

As they rode to the store, they went past kids with kites and kids with jump ropes. They went past a lake. They got the things on Mom's note.

When they got home, Pete and Jane broke the eggs. "Next you must mix up the lime cake and slide it into the stove to bake" said Mom.

"Let's ice it in white," said Pete. Then we can write on it."

"It is so cute," said Jane. "Dad will like it!"

When Dad got home, he said, "My nose smells cake."

Mom cut him a huge slice. She put it on a plate. A smile lit up Dad's face. "Yum! It has a nice taste. I'd like more.

Three Words

Write three words that tell what Dad's cake was like.

1. _____

2. _____

3. _____

What Do You See?

Write the name of each picture. If you hear a long sound, remember to use the VCe pattern.

_____

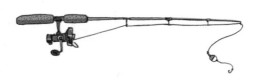

_____

_____

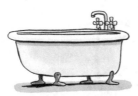

_____

_____

Primary Spelling by Pattern Student

_____

_____

_____

_____

_____

_____

_____

_____

_____

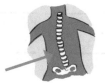

_____

Sentence Dictation

Write the words in the sentences your teacher says.

Be on the lookout for ck words and Floss words.

1. _____ , _____ .

2. _____ .

3. _____ .

4. _____ W _____ .

5. _____ .

Heart Words

1. _____

2. _____

3. _____

4. _____

5. _____

6. _____

7. _____

8. _____

9. _____

10. _____

11. _____

12. _____

13. _____

14. _____

15. _____

16. _____

17. _____

Remember your memory clues.

Giant in the City!

Say these words. Circle or highlight **ce**, **ci**, or **cy**.

cent	city	ace	rice	duce	face	nice

Copy these words.

1. race _____

2. trace _____

3. rice _____

4. space _____

5. dice _____

6. grace _____

7. spice _____

8. place _____

9. price _____

10. slice _____

11. face _____

12. twice _____

13. mice _____

14. race _____

15. ice _____

Word Sort

How is /s/ spelled? Write each word from the list in its column.

Word List

toss	suds	cell	chess	sack
cinch	cyber	cent	city	cycle

s

1. _____
2. _____

ss

1. _____
2. _____

ce

1. _____
2. _____

ci

1. _____
2. _____

cy

1. _____
2. _____

Speed Read

Underline **ce**, **ci**, and **cy** in the words below, as fast as you can. Read the words to yourself. Remember to read an /s/ sound for the letter **c**.

circus	cent	rice	
ace	cyclone	duce	
cinch	splice	cyber	
cycle	trace	cider	
center	cell	city	pace
recess	twice	place	juice

The letter c is sometimes used to spell the /s/ sound.

Lesson 17 Giant in the City (Soft *g*)

Reading and Spelling Words With Soft *g*

Say these words.

giant	gee	gym
age	huge	stage

Underline the **ge**, **gi**, or **gy**. What sound does the **g** make? _____

Say these words.

girl	get	gift

Underline the **g**. What sound does the **g** make? _____

Say these words.

| age | huge | dodge | bridge | page | sledge | cage | stage | sludge |

Underline the **dge** or **ge**. What sound does **dge** make? _____

Is it a dge or a ge at the end of a word ending in the sound /j/?

Primary Spelling by Pattern Student

Word Sort: Soft *g* and Hard *g*

After your teacher reads a word from the word list, write it in the column for the sound /g/ or /j/.

Word List

~~get~~	~~gee~~	gut	gym	gobs
ridge	rig	trudge	dug	egg
giant	grab	page	gloss	green
gift	gerbil			

The letter g is sometimes used to spell the /j/ sound.

Hard *g*: /g/	Soft *g*: /j/
get	gee

Read and Copy

Read each word, then copy it on the line. Underline **ge**, **gi**, and **gy** when they occur.

1. giant

2. gent

3. gym

4. germ

5. gin

6. age

7. page

8. stage

9. huge

10. rage

11. fudge

12. dodge

13. badge

14. pledge

15. ridge

Speed Read

Underline **ge**, **gi**, **gy**, **ce**, **ci**, and **cy** in the words below as fast as you can.

ace	fudge	cyclone	giant	cell	pace
gent	stage	circus	cyber	city	ridge
Cindy	cinch	splice	dodge	gentle	Gerry
rice	gym	center	dice	huge	
recess	age	place	cent	pledge	

How many words can you read?

_____

Spelling in Sound Boxes

Put the letters that spell each sound in the boxes. Highlight the *Giant in the City* patterns.

1.				
2.				
3.				
4.				
5.				
6.				
7.				
8.				
9.				
10.				
11.				
12.				
13.				
14.				
15.				
16.				
17.				
18.				

Sentence Dictation

Write the sentences after your teacher says them.

1. _____ could

Remember
to use dge
after a
short-vowel
sound.

2. _____ cream.

3. _____ .

4. _____ you _____ ?

5. _____

_____ ?

6. _____ you _____ ,

you _____ .

Lesson 18 Review

Dictation

Write the missing words in the sentences as your teacher says them.

1. _____ _____ _____
   _____ _____ _____ girl?
   _____ _____ _____ _____
   _____ _____ _____

   _____ _____ _____
   shiny _____ _____ _____ from
   _____ _____ _____ _____
   _____. _____

   _____ _____ _____
   _____ smooth _____ _____.
   _____ _____ _____
   _____ _____ _____ —,

   __ see _____!

2. My _____ _____ _____ _____ _____
_____ _____ _____ _____ _____ _____
_____ _____ _____ _____ _____ _____

woods. _____ _____ found _____ _____

tree. _____ _____ _____ _____

_____ _____ _____ _____

_____ _____ _____ _____

_____ _____ _____ _____

_____ _____ _____ . _____

_____ _____ _____ _____

_____ _____ , _____ _____

_____ _____ _____ _____

_____ , _____ _____ _____ _____

_____ _____ _____ !

_____ _____ _____ !

Alphabetical Order

a b c d e f g h i j k l m n o p q r s t u v w x y z

Write the words in the word list in alphabetical order on the lines below.

will	alone	not	when	like	just
so	family	have	was	could	good

1. _____

2. _____

3. _____

4. _____

5. _____

6. _____

7. _____

8. _____

9. _____

10. _____

11. _____

12. _____

Spelling in Sound Boxes

Listen for the sounds in each word your teacher says. Repeat the word. Stretch the sounds and write the letters for each sound in the boxes. Each box stands for one sound. Some sounds are spelled with more than one letter.

1.					
2.					
3.					
4.					
5.					
6.					
7.					
8.					
9.					
10.					
11.					
12.					
13.					
14.					
15.					
16.					

Visual Editing

Choose the correct spelling of the word your teacher says.

1.	frende	friend	frend	friende
2.	hoo	whow	who	hwo
3.	give	giv	giev	gice
4.	they	thay	tha	tey
5.	bace	back	backe	bak
6.	sed	sede	said	sayd
7.	with	whith	wif	whiv
8.	whut	what	wut	whate

Word Sort: Long and Short Vowels

Say each word in the word list. Write the word where it belongs.

Word List

huge	have	give	dive	page	love
badge	came	ledge	here	white	fudge

Long-Vowel Words	**Short-Vowel Words**
1. _____	1. _____
2. _____	2. _____
3. _____	3. _____
4. _____	4. _____
5. _____	5. _____
6. _____	6. _____

Making Corrections

Find each spelling mistake and cover it with a label. Write the correct spelling on the label.

When Tim is 7, his frinds are going to have a party for him. They will giv him lots uv gifts. Thay will play games and have cack.

Lesson 19 Shy Guys (Vowel Teams *ea* and *ee*)

Word Sort

Listen to the vowel sound in the word your teacher says and write it in the correct column.

ck is used after a short vowel.

Apple	Echo	Itch	Octopus	Umbrella Up

Primary Spelling by Pattern Student

Presto Change-o

Write the short-vowel word your teacher says. Then add silent **e** to make a new word.

1. pin   pine

2. _____   _____

3. _____   _____

4. _____   _____

5. _____   _____

6. _____   _____

7. _____   _____

8. _____   _____

9. _____   _____

10. _____   _____

Meet the "Shy Guys"

Draw the "shy guys" in the boxes below.

Read and Copy

Say each word before you copy it.

1. keep
2. peak
3. dream
4. seeds
5. queen
6. sheet
7. eat
8. three
9. free
10. wheel
11. street
12. cheer
13. green
14. feed
15. keep
16. scream

17. feel
18. seem
19. bleed
20. peel
21. bee
22. cream
23. seal
24. cheap
25. stream
26. beak
27. street
28. year

> It is always fair to ask if a word is spelled with an ee or an ea.

Finding Long-e Words in Context

Read the story. Highlight the words that have the long-**e** sound spelled **ee**, **ea**, or **e**.

At the Beach

Last year, Mom and Lee went to the beach. Wags went, too. They had a picnic to eat and a pail to use in the sand.

At the beach, Lee said, "Will you teach me to swim?"

Mom said, "Yes, but not yet. We need to wait. We must have our meal. They did not sit on seats. They sat on the sand. They could see sailboats in the sea. They ate ham and green beans, and they drank tea. They each had a peach. Wags ate, too. He ate meat.

Then Lee said, "Will you teach me to swim?"

"Yes," said Mom. "But not yet. We will dig in the sand. We will fill up the pail. Mom and Lee dug a deep hole in the sand. Wags dug too. He got sand on Lee's feet.

Lee said, "Can we get wet yet? I need to clean the sand off my feet."

"Yes," said Mom. "See how I float. You can float, too. Kick your feet. Then you can swim."

Lee did swim. It was fun.

Wags swam too. He got Mom and Lee wet. Then it was time to go home. Lee was sad. Wags was sad, too.

Word Sort

Sort the words in "At the Beach" that have the long-**e** sound.

ee	ea	e

Lesson 20 Shy Guys (Vowel Teams *ai* and *oa*)

Word Sort: Long Vowels

When your teacher says a word, listen for the long vowel. Write it in the right column.

apron	eagle	ice cream	unicorn	oval
Write the two /ē/ "shy guys" vowel teams here:				
What other way do we spell long vowels?				

Sentence Dictation

Write the sentences your teacher dictates.

1. _____ _____ _____ _____

    _____ _____ _____ _____ •

2. _____ _____ _____

    _____ _____ _____ _____

    _____ •

Did you remember the s on the end of two words?

Circle the "shy guys" vowel teams.

Read and Copy

Some words that sound the same have different spellings and meanings.

1. goat _____

2. train _____

3. pail* _____

4. road _____

5. goal _____

6. plain* _____

7. coat _____

8. chain _____

9. rain* _____

10. soap _____

11. tail* _____

12. boat _____

13. toad _____

14. drain _____

15. wait* _____

16. brain _____

17. throat _____

18. mail* _____

Dictation

Write the sentences as your teacher says them.
The quotation marks show that someone is talking.
Remember to start your sentences with uppercase letters.

Mom said,
"Sally's apple
is delicious!"

1. _____ _____ , _____ _____ "

   "
   _____ _____ _____ .

2. "
   _____ _____ _____ _____ _____ , "

   _____ _____ .

3. _____ teacher _____ , " ____ ____ _____

   "
   _____ _____ .

4. " _____ _____ , " _____

   _____ _____ .

Do you
need to ask
a question?

5. _____ _____ _____ , " ____

   "
   _____ _____ _____ _____ .

Reading

Read this story to yourself. Circle the "shy guys" **ee, ea, ai, oa**.

_____

Mike and His Black Goat

Mike has a cute black goat with a beard. His goat sleeps in a green shed near the road. Each week Mike has to help clean the shed. The goat likes to eat a lot of funny things. He eats rope and soap. He eats cans of paint and seaweed. He eats roast beef and wire. If you ate that stuff, you would feel sick. Each year Mike takes his goat to the fair. He wins a lot of prizes.

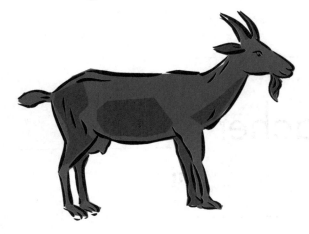

Reread the story. Write the action words that end with the letter **s**.

1. _____

2. _____

3. _____

4. _____

Dictation

Write the words as your teacher says them. Ask fair questions if you need to.

_____ _____ _____ _____ beard. _____

_____ _____ _____ _____ _____

funny _____ . _____ _____

_____ _____ _____ _____ _____

_____ _____ . _____ _____ _____

_____ _____ .

Words I Missed

1. _____   3. _____

2. _____   4. _____

You might want to ask about "shy guys" spellings and whether to use s or z.

Lesson 21 A Triple Header (Sounds of Final *y*)

Final-*y* Song

Listen as your teacher sings this song to you.

Final y Song

Final **y** can say $\bar{\text{i}}$
In little words like **my** and **cry**,
Don't be shy, give a try—
    the words **fly by**,
Final **y** can say $\bar{\text{i}}$

Final **y** can say $\bar{\text{a}}$
When the **y** comes after **a**
Play and **day** and **may** and **say**
Final **y** can spell $\bar{\text{a}}$

Final **y** can say $\bar{\text{e}}$
In longer words
Just look and see
Tiny, **happy**, **baby**, **sleepy** as can be
Final **y** can say $\bar{\text{e}}$

Primary Spelling by Pattern Student

Supported Writing

Write a rhyming poem. See how many **y** words you can use.

by cry dry fly my fry pry shy sly sky spy try why

_____

_____

_____

_____

_____

_____

_____

_____

_____

_____

Final y Song

Write eight **ay** words.

1. _____

2. _____

3. _____

4. _____

5. _____

6. _____

7. _____

8. _____

Word Sort

Sort the final-**y** words in the word list by their last vowel sound.

Word List

play	fly	baby	money	they	gray	puppy
candy	shy	lazy	stray	jay	glassy	funny
sleepy	why	creamy	rocky	nutty	pray	cry

long i /ī/	long a /ā/	long e /ē/
_____	_____	_____
_____	_____	_____
_____	_____	_____
_____	_____	_____
_____	_____	_____
_____	_____	_____
_____	_____	_____
_____	_____	_____
_____	_____	_____
_____	_____	_____

At Home in the City

_____ ___ ___ ___ ___ ___

_____ ___ ___ ___ ___ many people

_____•___ ___ ___ ___ _____ ___

_____ ___ ___ ___ ___ ___ • ___

_____ ___ ___ ___ ___ • ___

'
s

_____ ___ ___ ___ ___ ___ ___

_____ ___ ___ • ___ ___ ___

_____ ___ ___ ___ • ___

_____ ___ ___ ___ ___ _____•

It's fair to ask for help deciding how to spell long vowels.

Lesson 22 More and More (Plurals)

Picture This

Pretend that you own a toy store, and you want to make signs for the shelves. Write the plural for each toy on the sign beside it.

1. _____

2. _____

3. _____

4. _____

5. _____

Primary Spelling by Pattern Student

6. _____

7. _____

8. _____

9. _____

10. _____

Word Sort: Plurals

Sort the words in the word list by the spelling of their ending. Then add **es** to make them mean more than one.

Word List

glass	pitch	crash	fox	ditch	ash
ax	kiss	rash	mess	dress	pizza
street	plate	boss	itch	box	brush
inch	speech	wish	teacher	mix	

s or ss	ch or tch	sh
_____	_____	_____
_____	_____	_____
_____	_____	_____
_____	_____	_____
_____	_____	_____
_____	_____	_____

x	other
_____	_____
_____	_____
_____	_____
_____	_____
_____	_____

Spelling Plurals

Write the plural of each word.

1. baby _____

2. city _____

3. copy _____

4. daddy _____

5. penny _____

6. party _____

7. fairy _____

8. weekday _____

9. daisy _____

10. jelly _____

11. spy _____

12. turkey _____

13. fly _____

14. jelly _____

15. hobby _____

16. bunny _____

17. ray _____

18. try _____

19. cavity _____

20. okay _____

Check to see whether a vowel or a consonant comes before the final y. If it's a consonant, change the y to i and then add es. If it is a vowel, just add s.

Dictation

Listen, repeat, and write the sentences your teacher says.

1. _____ _____ _____ _____ _____ _____

   _____ _____ _____ _____ _____ •

2. _____ _____ _____ _____ _____

   _____ _____ _____ _____ _____

   _____ _____ _____ •

3. _____ _____ _____ _____ _____

   _____ _____ _____ _____ •

4. _____ _____ _____ _____ _____

   _____ _____ _____ _____ •

5. _____ _____ _____ _____ _____

_____ _____ _____ _____ _____

_____ _____ .

6. _____ _____ _____ _____ _____ _____

_____ _____ _____ _____

_____ _____ _____ .

7. _____ _____ _____ _____ _____

_____ _____ _____ _____ .

Still Needs Work:

- ☐ short vowel
- ☐ floss
- ☐ digraphs
- ☐ consonant blends
- ☐ **ng**
- ☐ **v**
- ☐ VCe
- ☐ **ce** giants
- ☐ shy guys
- ☐ final **y**
- ☐ plurals
- ☐ **ge** giants

Lesson 23 Let There Be Light

Which One Looks Right?

Listen to the word your teacher reads. Circle the correct spelling of the word.

1. chilldren   childrene   children

2. babes   babies   babys

3. dutterfly   butterli   butterfly

4. friend   frende   frend

5. love   luv   luve

6. dress   drese   dres

7. wishs   wishes   wises

8. train   chrain   tain

9. baf   bav   bath

10.	school	skool	school
11.	cande	candy	candie
12.	shop	chop	shope
13.	family	famuly	familie
14.	blac	black	blak
15.	sity	city	citee
16.	paj	page	paig
17.	plai	playe	play
18.	of	off	uv
19.	use	yous	youse
20.	going	goin	goung

Dictation: Lightbulb Words

Write the words your teacher says. Two of the words are spelled with **ite**.
Can you figure out which two?

1. _____   11. _____

2. _____   12. _____

3. _____   13. _____

4. _____   14. _____

5. _____   15. _____

6. _____   16. he _____

7. _____   17. eye _____

8. _____   18. _____

9. _____   19. _____

10. _____   20. all— _____

Words With *kn*

Words with **kn** are some of the oldest in English. Learn this poem to know what some of them are. Underline the words with **kn**.

Knowledge

Once, long ago, there was a knight

who knew he needed knowledge.

He packed some knockwurst into his knapsack,

and headed off to college.

He took along his knitted socks,

to warm his knobby knees,

He bought some books, and knuckled down,

to learn his ABC's.

Memory Clue	Heart Word

Here's a trick to help you remember how to spell **knight** and **night**:

The <u>k</u>night works for the <u>k</u>ing.

Is it an
n or a kn?

know

Fill in the Blanks

Use lightbulb words with **ight**.

Word List

bright	fight	fright	flight
kite	light	night	might
plight	right	sight	tight
slight	midnight	flashlight	**he**ight
eyesight	skintight	bite	**all**-night

The Knight's Misunderstanding

Dwight was a _____ with bad _____. He wore

armor that was _____. One _____ he had an awful

_____ because he forgot to turn on his _____.

It was about _____ and there was no _____

when he caught _____ of two _____ eyes staring at him from

a _____ of about thirty feet. "This is not right," said Dwight, the

_____. He ran off in _____. He bumped into a princess dressed

in a _____ pink party dress. She looked lovely in the _____.

"Why are you _____?" asked the princess.

"The knight, said "I think I _____ have seen a

terrible monster with eyes as big as _____.

The princess was _____ scared, but she said bravely,

"I'd be _____ to _____ the monster for you."

"All _____," said Dwight. They set off at _____.

Dwight pointed to two _____ yellow eyes staring at

them through the _____.

Shaking in _____, Dwight hid behind the princess.

She grabbed the _____ and turned it on. She aimed

the _____ in the direction of the huge, scary eyes. Then she

started to laugh. "Look," she said. "Those are not monster eyes. That is just

_____ shining from two upstairs castle windows."

"You are _____, said Dwight. I was not very _____!"

Then he added, "I'd be _____ if you'd stop

for a snack with me at the _____ diner.

Lesson 24 Review

Dictation: Heart Word Sentences

Listen, repeat, and write the three sentences
your teacher says.

1. _____'s _____

_____ _____

_____ _____ _____

_____ _____ _____ .

2. _____ _____ _____ _____ .

3. _____ _____ _____ _____

_____ _____ _____ .

Partners

Practice spelling these fair words with a partner.

can	this	long
and	it	when
at	his	why
had	did	tell
am	him	off

as	will	way	make
that	its	he	made
when	with	she	time
may	which	we	more
get	if	so	have

them	not	be	live
then	on	no	see
when	up	use	each
is	but	these	by
in	just	like	my

Alphabetical Order

a b c d e f g h i j k l m n o p q r s t u v w x y z

Put the words in the word list in alphabetical order.

Word List

| sent | right | just | gem | cent | night | write | knight |

Write the words in the word list in alphabetical order on the lines below.

1. _____   5. _____

2. _____   6. _____

3. _____   7. _____

4. _____   8. _____

Write the right word in each sentence. Use the words from the word list above.

1. When I look to the _____, I can see my school.

2. He can _____ his name.

3. I have a _____ in my ring.

4. Was the letter _____ in the mail?

5. We stayed up all _____.

6. They came home _____ in time for lunch.

Word Unscramble

Use the letters below to make real words.

1. antw _____

2. hwree _____

3. reew _____

4. wath _____

5. chwhi _____

6. hwne _____

7. thiw _____

8. hwy _____

Spelling in Sound Boxes

Each box stands for one sound. Some sounds are spelled with two or more letters. Write the letters that spell each sound.

1. **soap**					
2. **float**					
3. **roam**					
4. **trains**					
5. **stray**					
6. **today**					
7. **tricks**					
8. **treat**					
9. **beaches**					
10. **wishes**					

Snowflake Words With ow

Write the words in the right column after your teacher writes them on the board.

ow	Other (o, o_e, oe, ough)
snow blow row	go toe owe though

Fill in the Blanks

Use the words you wrote above to fill in the blanks.

1. In the winter it may _____.

2. In summer there is grass to _____.

3. When we go to watch a _____, we like to sit in the front _____.

4. We plant seeds and hope they'll _____.

5. We guard the plants with a scare _____.

6. And I bet you all _____ that fires _____ and rivers _____.

7. You shoot arrows with a _____.

8. When cars break down, they need a _____.

9. You can swing high, and you can swing _____.

10. When you greet friends, you say _____.

11. You say good-by when it's time to _____.

12. The opposite of **above** is _____.

13. The opposite of **yes** is _____.

If you're not sure which long o spelling to use, it's fair to ask.

Word Sort: Long Vowels

Write the words in the word list in the correct column.

Word List

tail	chime	monkey	might	throw	slow
gray	chair	nose	whale	soap	shy
sleep	stream	shake	pretty	bright	fright
tight	those	grow	snow	night	blow

VCe	"Shy Guys" ee | ea ai | oa	Final y y = /ī/ y = /ā/ y = /ē/	Lightbulb Pattern	Snowflake Pattern

Contractions

Put the two words together and write the contraction. Read the sentence.

can + not = _____   I **can't** throw this away.

he + will = _____   We hope **he'll** come with us.

she + is = _____   She thinks **she's** the best.

we + are = _____   **We're** so happy that Dad is home.

he + is = _____   **He's** very fast.

I + am = _____   **I'm** damp from the rain.

I + have = _____   **I've** lost my glasses.

let + us = _____   **Let's** go play in the snow.

Apostrophe Rhyme

When two words bump together,

some letters disappear.

Apostrophe's the substitute

who comes to volunteer.

Story Dictation

Write the story as your teacher reads it.

The Three Bears

Once _____ _____

_____ bears. _____

bear, _____ bear _____.

_____ _____ _____ _____ porridge,

_____," _____. _____

_____

porridge _____. _____

gone, Goldilocks _____ _____

_____ house. _____ _____ ed _____

_____ door, _____ one _____, so

_____ _____ _____. _____ _____ _____ _____ bear

_____ 's chair _____ _____ _____. _____

_____ bear _____ 's porridge. _____

upstairs _____ _____ _____ bears _____

"
_____ _____. _____ _____ _____

"
_____ _____ _____ _____ _____ _____, _____

Goldilocks, " _____ _____ _____ _____ care."

_____ bear _____ 's

_____ _____ _____ _____. _____ _____ bears

_____ _____, _____ were _____ ! _____

chased Goldilocks _____ _____

house." _____ !" _____ed

_____ bears.

Lesson 26 The Terrible Twenty

Memory Clue for w Words

Read the words in the word list. Underline the words that start with **wh**. What kind of words start with **wh**?

When in doubt, leave h out.

Word List

when	watch	who	were	where	week
went	which one	warm	wind	what	wait
wife	wish	why	while	want	whole

Fill in the Blanks

Write the missing word after your teacher reads the sentence.

1. _____ will he play with me?

2. I'm here for a whole _____.

3. _____ are we going?

4. Make a _____ and blow!

5. Don't _____; you'll be late.

6. My _____ is here with me.

7. _____ this and not that?

8. Let's eat _____ we wait.

9. _____ do you think you are?

10. I ate the _____ piece of pie.

Alphabetical Order: w Words

abcdefghijklmnopqrstuvwxyz

All the words in the word list start with **w**. Look at the second letter to alphabetize them.

Word List

was   what   were   will   words   write

1. _____   4. _____

2. _____   5. _____

3. _____   6. _____

Memory Clues

Write the memory sentence for each word. Your teacher will help you.

want   1. _____

were   2. _____

went   3. _____

Heart Words

Write the memory clue for each Heart Word.

from   1. _____

first   2. _____

people   3. _____

water   4. _____

The three
there's always
start with
t-h-e.

The Three There's

Think about the spellings of the word **there**. Read each sentence, and circle the correct one.

1. The boys rode (**there, their, they're**) bikes.

2. Put your homework (**there, their, they're**), on the table.

3. If they don't run, (**there, their, they're**) going to miss the bus.

4. In the summer (**there, their, they're**) going to travel to visit

   (**there, their, they're**) grandmother.

Editing

There are 15 mistakes in this short story. Put a label over each error and write the correct spelling on the label.

The Shopping Trip

Mom sed, "I hav to go shopping. You kids can come whith me. Ferst we will get sum things for lunch. Then u can each pick a treat."

There were meny peple at the store, but it didnt' take long for them to get the things thay needed.

Mom asked, "Whut do you wont to get?"

The kids picked grapes and a bag uv chips Then it wus time to go home form the store.

Lesson 27 Sailboats and Sandboxes

Word Sort: Contractions and Compounds

Write each word from the word list in the correct column.

Word List

drumstick	cupcake
pretend	don't
isn't	dislike
sunshine	unhappy
aren't	we'll
mealtime	

Contractions	Compound Words	Other
_____	_____	_____
_____	_____	_____
_____	_____	_____
_____	_____	_____

Do You Hear What I Hear?

Listen to each compound word as your teacher says it. Write the vowel sounds you hear in each "free" word of the compound.

Example: sunlight __ŭ__ , __ī__

1. _____ , _____

2. _____ , _____

3. _____ , _____

4. _____ , _____

5. _____ , _____

6. _____ , _____

7. _____ , _____

8. _____ , _____

9. _____ , _____

10. _____ , _____

11. _____ , _____

12. _____ , _____

13. _____ , _____

14. _____ , _____

15. _____ , _____

Building Compound Words

Combine the "free" words in the list into as many compound words as you can. Write them on the lines below.

Word List

day	time	night	fire	man	snow	bed
house	sun	light	up	down	town	

_____

_____

_____

_____

What's Wrong Here?

Many of the following words are spelled incorrectly. Write them as they should be spelled. Remember that in compound words, we spell each word just as it would be if the "free" words were not connected. If a word is correct, you don't have to write it again.

1. storebook _____

2. daylight _____

3. anewhere _____

4. cribaby _____

5. candebar _____

6. butterfly _____

7. kittilitter _____

8. plaground _____

Picture This: Compound Words

How many things can you think of that are compound words? Draw at least five in a picture in the frame below. Write the compound words you've illustrated on the lines below the picture.

My Compound Words

_____

_____

_____

Dictation

Listen, ask questions, and write the sentences your teacher says. Words you haven't studied are written for you.

1. _____ _____ _____ _____ _____ _____ _____

_____ _____ jogged _____ _____ _____ .

2. _____ _____ _____ _____ _____

_____ _____ _____ _____ .

3. _____ _____ _____er _____ _____

_____ _____ _____ _____ _____ .

4. _____ _____ _____ _____ _____

_____ _____ _____ _____ .

5. _____ _____ _____

every_____ .

6. ___ _____ _____ _____ _____ _____

   _____ _____ _____ ____ _____ _____.

7. _____ _____ _____ ed _____ ____ _____

   _____ ____ er _____ ____ ____ _____.

8. _____ _____ ____ _____ ____ ___ frozen

   _____ _____ ___ _____ _____.

9. _____ _____ ___ _____ _____ for____

   _____ _____ ___ _____ _____.

Still Needs Work:

☐ short vowel   ☐ floss   ☐ digraphs   ☐ consonant blends

☐ **ng**   ☐ **v**   ☐ VCe   ☐ **ce** giants

☐ shy guys   ☐ final **y**   ☐ plurals   ☐ **ge** giants

Lesson 28 Ouch

Read and Copy

1. ouch _____

2. about _____

3. how _____

4. house _____

5. shout _____

6. now _____

7. our _____

8. out _____

9. down _____

10. brown _____

11. owl _____

12. proud _____

13. pound _____

14. growl _____

15. sound _____

16. cloud _____

17. found _____

18. town _____

19. ground _____

20. towel _____

Primary Spelling by Pattern Student

Word Sort

Write each "ouch" word in the list in the correct column based on the where the /ou/ sound occurs in the word. The first five are done for you. Do you see any patterns in the spelling of the words?

Word List

frown	sound	growl	ouch	now	owl
cow	clown	proud	prowl	shout	fowl
scout	pound	down	how	wow	clown
found	howl	about	out	towel	cloud
house	town	our	ounce	plow	

End	Before n	Before nd/d	Before l or el	Before t, ch, r, nce, or se
now	frown	sound	growl	ouch

Finding /ou/ Words in Context

Read the story. With a light-colored crayon, cross out each word that has **ou** or **ow**. Can you find 34 words?

Loud Sounds

Once this planet was not such a loud place. Trout swam soundlessly in the streams and owls flew around in the air above the ground. People plowed the land by hand. Now power tractors do the plowing. Long ago, people did not have CD players in their houses. Now just about everybody does. Today everyone lives crowded into towns and big cities. A brown cloud floats above the places where people work, and countless sounds fill the air. People are even shouting more. You can't go anywhere without hearing sounds that can hurt your ears. People who study sound, counted how many loud sounds we hear every day. They were astounded at what they found. They say that we must somehow come up with rules to cut down on the mounting amount of sound that is making our planet such a loud place.

Finding Homophones in Context: Sound Alikes

Read the sentences for each word pair and underline the two words that sound alike.

Ask which spelling to use.

1. **flour, flower**

   Mom mixed the flour with the eggs in the bowl.
   José gave his teacher a yellow flower.

2. **bare, bear**

   Addie had bare feet when she waded in the stream.
   We saw a black bear at the zoo.

3. **board, bored**

   I pounded a nail into the board.
   I was bored when it rained all day.

4. **dear, deer**

   Mom's dear friend e-mails her every week.
   A deer bounded past us.

5. **groan, grown**

   People groan if they lift big boxes.
   My teacher said, "My, but you have grown."

6. **here, hear**

   Here is my coat.
   Did you hear me calling?

7. **maid, made**

   The maid cleaned the motel.
   I made cupcakes for my friend.

8. **one, won**

   I ate just one candy.
   The best player won the game.

9. **red, read**

   He had a red jacket for snowy days.
   We read a lot of books in first grade.

10. **right, write**

    I think I have the right answer.
    I write with my white pencil.

Sentence Writing

Use the two words in a good sentence. Your sentence can be a question.

1. **would, you**

   _____

   _____

   _____

2. **flour, ground**

   _____

   _____

   _____

3. **house, crowded**

   _____

   _____

   _____

4. **sound, loud**

   _____

   _____

   _____

5. **should, shouldn't**

   _____

   _____

   _____

Primary Spelling by Pattern Student

Do You Hear What I Hear?

Listen to the word your teacher says. Circle the word with the same vowel sound.

1.	home	lake	stamp
2.	round	trap	life
3.	make	slip	too
4.	hid	bike	coat
5.	face	feel	ouch
6.	boy	give	seem
7.	chair	close	much
8.	long	best	the
9.	mine	think	tell
10.	who	said	just
11.	where	sum	to

Finding /ū/ Words in Context

Highlight or underline all the words with the New Moon sound spelled **ew** or **oo**.

The Moose and the Moon

One night, Little Moose woke up from a snooze. He knew that he should stay near Mama Moose, but he wanted some food, so he went off to find something to chew on. The moon was bright, and he was sure he would not lose his way.

Little Moose had only eaten a few roots when a loon flew down and hooted at him. The wind blew. Little Moose remembered Mother Moose's warning that hunters might shoot if they saw a moose. "A moose running loose," she had said, "might get put in a zoo."

The air grew cooler. The sky grew darker and gloomier. Little Moose heard the BOOM, BOOM, BOOM of thunder! The moon disappeared. "Boo hoo," said Little Moose. I'm doomed. The moon is gone. I need a new moon so that I can find my way home to Mama Moose."

Just then, the moon called, "You-hoo! Here I am. I was just playing peek-a-boo with the clouds."

"Whew!" said Little Moose. "I was worried."

Just then, a rooster cock-a-doodle-dooed.

"Oh, no," said Little Moose. "Mama will wake up and notice that I am missing. Toodle-oo," he called, as he vamoosed back to Mama.

Mama Moose was so glad to see Little Moose that she gave him a smooch. Then she told him that running off by himself was a foolish thing to do.

Read and Copy—and Color

In each row, color the first box to match the color word. Write the color word four times in the boxes that follow it.

red				
blue				
yellow				
green				
purple				
orange				
brown				
black				
pink				
white				

Rhyme Time

Fill in the blanks in the rhyme puzzles below.

We're off into space. We won't get there soon. It takes a long time to fly to the _____.	When you're crabby, and in a bad mood, sometimes you just need a little _____.
Santa flies through the night. He lands on a roof; then we hear the prancing of each reindeer _____.	Because he ate so much bamboo, the little panda grew and _____.
They have pockets and live in zoos. You're right if you said they're _____.	Jackson liked his mama's noodles, So she always cooked him _____.
Mom calls me loudly, "Please get a broom. Before you go play, you must clean this _____."	Don't you know that it's a rule? Kids can't chew gum in _____.
Dad shakes his head "The day's too cool, to go for a swim in the outdoor _____."	He prowls at night. He sleeps till noon. His eyes are black. He's a _____.

 142

Fill in the Blanks—and Draw

Complete the sentence in each box with your own idea. Draw a picture for each sentence.

Box 1 I like **to** _____ .

Box 2 I have **too** many _____ .

Box 3 The playground has swings and _____ , **too**.

Box 4 I have **two** _____ .

Lesson 30 Cookbook (o͞o)

Poem

Listen to your teacher read the poem. Listen for all the words with the /o͞o/-**look** sound.

I'm Hooked

I'm hooked.

I took my fishing pole and hook.

Then I walked down beside the brook.

I stood,

and stood,

and stood,

and stood.

The fishing wasn't very good.

I almost went to read a book.

Instead I took my pole and hook,

and walked on farther down the brook.

I looked,

and looked,

and looked,

and looked.

And suddenly my pole, it shook.

"A fish, a fish!" I cried, "Oh look!"

Come take a picture for my book.

Contraction Action

Write the two words for each contraction.

wouldn't _____   would've _____

couldn't _____   could've _____

shouldn't _____   should've _____

Spelling Words With Qu

Write the words that start with **qu**.

 qu ___ ___ ___    sq ___ ___ ___ ___

 qu ___ ___ ___   sq ___ ___ ___ ___

 qu ___ ___ ___    qu ___ ___ ___ ___

 qu ___ ___ ___    qu ___ ___ ___ ___ ___ ___

 qu ___ ___ruplets

Qu Words

Write the **qu** word for each definition.

1. The wife of a king. _____

2. The sound made by a duck. _____

3. A small test. _____

4. Another word for fast. _____

5. When you give up before finishing. _____

Additional Qu Words

_____

_____

Dictation: Word Sort

Listen, repeat, and write each word in the right column.

Short Vowels	Long Vowels	Other Vowels
_____	_____	_____
_____	_____	_____
_____	_____	_____
_____	_____	_____
_____	_____	_____
_____	_____	_____
_____	_____	_____
_____	_____	_____
_____	_____	_____

Lesson 31 Who Let the Pigs In?

Oi **and** Oy **Words**

Copy the words you wrote with the class on the board.

oi	oy
boil	boy

Word Detective

Write the words that answer these questions.

1. Another name for a penny, quarter, or nickel: _____

2. When food goes bad in the heat: _____

3. The opposite of girl: _____

4. To take pleasure in an activity: _____

5. What we speak with: _____

6. To give someone a job: _____

7. To put two parts together: _____

8. What I put into my car engine: _____

Word Sort

What kind of word? Write each word in the word list in the correct column.

Word Bank

green	ran	haystack	huge	quit	long
nailed	nighttime	moon	whine	trout	white

Describing Words	Action Words	Words for Things
bright	playing	snowflake
_____	_____	_____
_____	_____	_____
_____	_____	_____

Fill in the Blanks

Complete each sentence by writing the missing part of the compound word.

1. The witch flew around town on her _____ stick .

2. I like _____ made cookies better than ones you buy in the store.

3. In the computer lab, we type on the _____ board .

4. Tai stayed the _____ end at her grandmother's house.

5. The first-graders went out to the _____ ground for recess.

6. On the Fourth of July, the whole family watched the _____ works over the lake.

7. The soccer players won because they used such good _____ work .

8. Grandma put up her umbrella when the _____ drops began falling.

9. Baby Katy put her yellow duck in the _____ tub .

10. When the power went off, Dad rushed to get a _____ light .

11. Luke put on his mittens so that he could go out and make _____ balls .

12. The cow_____ wore chaps and boots.

13. Dad said, "Look, the deer left a _____ print in the snow."

14. The girls played jump_____ out front.

15. The red lady_____ had lots of black spots on it.

Finding Words in Context:
New Moon, /o͝o/-look, /o/-snowflake, and /oi/-oink

Find the words from the word list in the puzzle and circle them.

Word List

too	so	boy	look	brown
down	wow	boo	hoop	oil
grown	tools	sound	noise	toy
join	bow	noon	point	flow
loop	shoot	snow	joy	crow

A Z B T K L W Y S N O W C G B

L S O U N D L N O I S E O R P

T O Y X J O I N G L V E P O Q

O U A B O W W B S J O H Z W E

O I Y R T N O O N M P O I N T

R Q L O E Y W O B V U O R K O

F L O W X S T F L O O P X Y O

R O I N S H O O T Q S L O K L

Z O J F W H Q P W O E O I I S

T K J O Y U C R O W T X L N H

Number Words

Write the number words. Write the memory clue for each word that does not follow a pattern.

1. _one_   _There is only one bird on the nest._

2. _____ _____

3. _____

4. _____ _____

5. _____

6. _____

7. _____

8. _____ _____

9. _____ _____

10. _____ _____

Counting Creatures

Color the animals. Write the number, color, and name of each animal on the lines beside the picture.

number	color	name

1. _____ _____ _____

2. _____ _____ _____

3. _____ _____ _____

4. _____ _____ _____

	number	color	name
5.	_____	_____	_____
6.	_____	_____	_____
7.	_____	_____	_____
8.	_____	_____	_____
9.	_____	_____	_____
10.	_____	_____	_____

Read and Copy

Read and copy these words.

aw		au	
draw		haul	
lawn		August	
raw		because	
law		auto	
saw		fault	
squawk		sauce	

al **or** all	
walk	
fall	
call	
tall	
talk	
ball	

au, aw, al, all

Aw... shucks!

Spelling Common /aw/ Words

Underline the vowels. Say the words. Count the syllables. Copy the words.

also	almost	altogether
_____	_____	_____

always	all right
_____	_____

Double Trouble: The Consonant Doubling Pattern

Break the following words into the base word and the ending. Drop the doubled consonant.

run<u>n</u>ing = _run_ + _ing_   hop<u>p</u>ed = _hop_ + _ed_

Base + Ending			Floss Words		
batting	= _bat_	+ _ing_	tossed	= _toss_	+ _ed_
stopped	= _stop_	+ _____	filling	= _____	+ _____
sunning	= _____	+ _____	stuffed	= _____	+ _____
stepping	= _____	+ _____	buzzed	= _____	+ _____
trimmed	= _____	+ _____	messy	= _____	+ _____
winner	= _____	+ _____	grassy	= _____	+ _____

In words with one short vowel followed by one consonant double the consonant before **ed**, **ing**, and **y**:

_____   _____   _____

Word Sort: Double Consonants

Sort the words in the word list. Write each word in the correct column. Think about the pattern they follow.

Word List

shouted	dawned	growled	smiled	crashed	dropped
slipped	grinned	kicked	screamed	oiled	called
slowed	hoped	milked	popped	clapped	melted
rained	pounded	dumped	camped	smoked	scrubbed

Base word has a short vowel followed by single consonant letter	Base word has a short vowel, but ends in more than one consonant letter
dropped	crashed

Word List

shouted	dawned	growled	smiled	crashed	dropped
slipped	grinned	kicked	screamed	oiled	called
slowed	hoped	milked	popped	clapped	melted
rained	pounded	dumped	camped	smoked	scrubbed

Base word has a long vowel	Base word has another vowel sound
hoped	oiled

Lesson 33 Bossy R

Dictation: Final-y Patterns

Fill in the blanks. Then, use your clues to spell the words your teacher dictates.

In a word where final y is the only vowel, y =

In a word where final y comes after a, y =

In a word with more than one syllable, final y =

1. _____

2. _____

3. _____

4. _____

5. _____

6. _____

7. _____

8. _____

9. _____

10. _____

11. _____

12. _____

13. _____

14. _____

15. _____

16. _____

17. _____

18. _____

19. _____

20. _____

21. _____

22. _____

23. _____

24. _____

25. _____

When we spell compound words, we spell each word as one word.

Remember the Heart Words.	
1. _____	3. _____
2. _____	4. _____

Sounds in Context

Read this poem and find all the **Bossy R** words.

Excuse Her

When Bossy R came for dinner.

We stuffed lots of food right in her,

Oranges, oysters, lobster, liver.

She'll eat anything you give her!

Parsnips, turkey, Harvard beets,

My, what funny things she eats,

Curried corn, and purple jello,

Celery, sherbet, a marshmallow.

We gave her turnips, tarts and more.

Then she headed for the door.

As she climbed into her car,

We fed her sardines from a jar.

She thanked us, waved and drove away,

That is when we heard her say,

"Burp."

Alphabetizing

a b c d e f g h i j k l m n o p q r s t u v w x y z

Notice that all the words in each group begin with the same two first letters. When you alphabetize them, you'll have to look beyond those letters, and put the words in order by the third letter.

chin	children	chapter	chart
chunk	chime	choose	cheat

1. _____

2. _____

3. _____

4. _____

5. _____

6. _____

7. _____

8. _____

shut	shine	shake	shower
shed	shirt	short	shoot

1. _____

2. _____

3. _____

4. _____

5. _____

6. _____

7. _____

8. _____

Continued on the next page.

abcdefghijklmnopqrstuvwxyz

| while | who | which | when |
| whale | what | why | where |

1. _____   5. _____

2. _____   6. _____

3. _____   7. _____

4. _____   8. _____

| think | third | three | thank |
| throw | thirty | thumb | there |

1. _____   5. _____

2. _____   6. _____

3. _____   7. _____

4. _____   8. _____

A Penny for Your Thoughts

Put a penny on the vowel sound that matches the vowel in the word your teacher says.

ou, ow	oi, oy	oo, ew, u_e, u, ou
au, aw, al, all	oo, u	er

Her Teacher

High-Frequency Words With Memory Clues

1. _____
2. _____
3. _____
4. _____
5. _____
6. _____
7. _____
8. _____
9. _____
10. _____
11. _____
12. _____
13. _____
14. _____
15. _____
16. _____

17. _____
18. _____
19. _____
20. _____
21. _____
22. _____
23. _____
24. _____
25. _____

1. _____
2. _____
3. _____
4. _____
5. _____
6. _____

Vowel-Bingo

Play a game of Bingo with your class.

V	O	W	E	L

Word Detective

Use the clues to solve these mysteries.

1. A past tense word spelled with **ed**: _____

2. An unfair past tense for **say**: _____

3. Two Old Uncle Larry words: _____

4. A pair of words that are opposites: _____

5. Three two-letter words that end in a long sound: _____

6. A Floss word: _____

7. An **ow** (ouch) word: _____

   An **ou** (ouch) word: _____

8. Three final-**y** words: _____

9. Two words that begin with /w/: _____

10. A word that follows the final -**ve** rule: _____

11. A Bossy **R** word spelled with **ir**: _____

12. A VCe word with three letters: _____

   With four letters: _____

   With five letters: _____

13. A word with the **ea** "shy guy": _____

14. An **ing**, **ang**, **ong** word: _____

15. Three unfair Heart Words: _____

16. A pair of homophones (words that sound the same but are spelled

    differently and have different meanings): _____

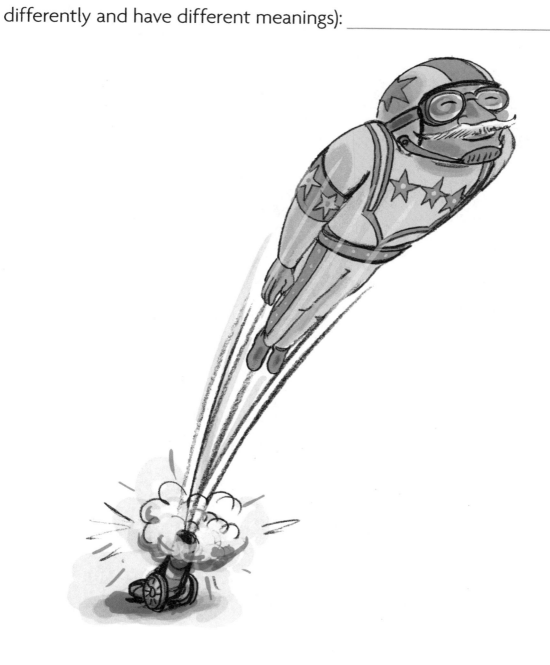

Final Paragraph Dictation

Start your sentences with capital letters.

_____

_____

_____

_____

_____

_____

_____

_____

_____

_____ _____ _____ , _____ _____ _____ _____

_____ _____ _____ _____ _____

_____ _____ _____ _____ .

_____ _____ _____ _____

_____ _____ _____ . _____ _____

_____ _____ _____ _____

_____ . _____ _____

_____ _____ _____ _____

_____ . _____ _____ _____

_____ _____ _____ .

CONGRATULATIONS!
You are a champion speller!

Vowel Patterns

Work with your teacher to fill in all the spaces on the vowel chart. Draw the pictures if you would like to.

Short-Vowel Patterns	Long-Vowel Patterns	Other-Vowel Patterns
1. _____	1. _____	1. _____
2. _____	2. _____	2. _____
3. _____	3. _____	3. _____
4. _____	4. _____	4. _____
5. _____	5. _____	5. _____
	6. _____	6. _____

Dictation

1. _____
2. _____
3. _____
4. _____
5. _____
6. _____
7. _____
8. _____
9. _____
10. _____
11. _____
12. _____

13. _____
14. _____
15. _____
16. _____
17. _____
18. _____
19. _____
20. _____
21. _____
22. _____
23. _____
24. _____

25. _____

26. _____

27. _____

28. _____

29. _____

30. _____

31. _____

32. _____

33. _____

34. _____

35. _____

36. _____

37. _____

38. _____

39. _____

The High-Frequency Word List

The 100 most frequently written words in the English language.

the	or	out	its
of	by	them	who
and	one	then	now
a	had	she	people
to	not	many	my
in	but	some	made
is	what	so	over
you	all	these	did
that	were	would	down
it	when	other	only
he	we	into	way
for	there	has	find
was	can	more	use
on	an	her	may
are	your	two	water
as	which	like	long
with	their	him	little
his	said	see	very
they	if	time	after
at	do	could	words
be	will	no	called
this	each	make	just
from	about	than	where
I	how	first	most
have	up	been	know